Muhammad ALI

Arlene Schulman

Lerner Publications Company
Minneapolis

*In memory of my father, Alan Schulman,
who shared a birthday with Muhammad Ali*

A&E and **BIOGRAPHY** are trademarks of the A&E Television Networks, registered in the United States and other countries.

Some of the people profiled in this series have also been featured in A&E's acclaimed BIOGRAPHY series, which is available on videocassette from A&E Home Video. Call 1-800-423-1212 to order.

Copyright © 2000 by Arlene Schulman
First published in 1996 by Lerner Publications Company under the title
Muhammad Ali: Champion.

First Avenue Editions
A division of Lerner Publishing Group
241 First Avenue North
Minneapolis, MN 55401 U.S.A.

Website address: www.lernerbooks.com

Library of Congress Cataloging-in-Publication Data

Schulman, Arlene.
    Muhammad Ali : / by Arlene Schulman.
      p.   cm. — (A&E biography)
    Includes bibliographical references (p.) and index.
    ISBN 0-8225-9693-8 (pbk.: alk. paper)
    1. Ali, Muhammad, 1942—Juvenile literature. 2. Boxers
(Sports)—United States—Biography—Juvenile literature.
[1. Ali, Muhammad, 1942– . 2. Boxers (Sports) 3. Afro-Americans—
Biography.] I. Title. II. Series
GV1132.A44 S367 2000
796.83'092—dc21
                                                                00-010280

Manufactured in the United States of America
1 2 3 4 5 6 – JR – 05 04 03 02 01 00

CONTENTS

Ali holds a diamond-studded belt naming him America's Professional Athlete of the Year for 1975.

CHAPTER ONE

THE
GREATEST

Float like a butterfly, sting like a bee
His hands can't hit what his eyes can't see
Now you see me, now you don't
George thinks he will, but I know he won't.

"GEORGE FOREMAN IS NOTHING BUT A BIG MUMMY," Muhammad Ali declared to reporters before the fight called the "Rumble in the Jungle." "George Foreman ain't nothing. He's a big old bully from Texas who used to beat up people in the streets."

Ali predicted that Foreman would lose. Clever and confident, Ali was right. Although the experts expected

Foreman to win the October 1974 world heavyweight championship fight in Kinshasa, Zaire, Ali knocked him out in the eighth round. Foreman used up most of his energy hitting Ali's arms and gloves—missing his head and body.

Ali taunted him before an exhausted Foreman ran out of energy. "Is that all you've got, Big George?" he asked in the middle of the fight. "Don't you know who I am?" Ali then knocked him out with a barrage of punches.

Muhammad Ali was a brash young man with a loud voice and a disarming sense of humor who became the heavyweight champion of the world three times. He used the boxing ring as his stage. He was light on his feet and moved quickly around the ring, dancing to the "Ali shuffle," skillfully bouncing off the ropes, and wearing down his opponents with a technique he called "rope-a-dope."

> I'LL SAY IT AGAIN, I'VE SAID IT BEFORE, ARCHIE MOORE WILL FALL IN FOUR.

He called himself "the Greatest" and knocked out men like Sonny Liston, Floyd Patterson, and George Foreman to prove it. He wrote witty lines of verse to describe his opponents, predicted the rounds in which they would fall, and then knocked them out.

His early backdrop was the turbulent 1960s—the civil rights movement, the women's rights movement, and protests against the Vietnam War. Ali opposed the war on religious grounds, refused to be inducted into the United States Army, and lectured about his political and

The young fighter tells the world: Sonny Liston will fall in the eighth round.

religious beliefs at college campuses from Harvard to Howard.

He became a Muslim just after he won his first heavyweight title, changing his name from Cassius Clay to Muhammad Ali—a move that many said would hurt his

Down goes Floyd Patterson, 1966.

career, but he did so anyway. Afterward, if an opponent called him Cassius Clay, he retaliated by hitting him even harder in the ring.

Ali captivated television viewers and sports reporters with his wit and charm. He was charismatic and outspoken—unusual for a black man in the 1960s and rare for a boxer—and people listened. He became a folk hero, a symbol of racial pride, and he was praised as a man who stood up for his beliefs.

He met presidents and heads of state, athletes and entertainers, but he always belonged to the public. Traveling around the world, from Africa to Indonesia to the Soviet Union, Ali was—and still is—recognized everywhere.

"I've seen a lot of fighters who want to be Muhammad Ali," said Eddie Futch, trainer of several champions. "But there's never been anyone who even comes close."

The future champ,
age 12, Louisville,
Kentucky

CHAPTER TWO

DREAMS OF GLORY

THEY WOULD SIT AT NIGHT, AND HE WOULD TELL her that he was going to be the champion of the world. In their ramshackle house in Louisville, Kentucky, when the sun had set and the lights were out, 12-year-old Cassius Clay told his mother of his dream. He would knock out opponents one by one, raise his hands in victory as the ring announcer introduced him as the new world champion, and become rich and famous.

"One night I heard [heavyweight champion] Rocky Marciano fighting on the radio," he said. "It sounded so big and powerful and exciting."

Cassius Marcellus Clay Jr. was born on January 17, 1942, in Louisville. The first of two sons born to Odessa Clay and Cassius Clay Sr., Cassius Jr. demonstrated his fondness for attention even at an early age. Mrs. Clay, exhausted from a difficult delivery, could hear her young son cry and scream and wake up the other babies in the hospital.

Clay's hometown of Louisville in the 1940s

"Gee-gee, gee-gee," were Cassius's first words, his mother said. He later claimed that he was trying to say "Golden Gloves," the name of a prestigious national boxing tournament that he won twice as a teenager. "When he was a child, he never sat still," his mother recalled. "He walked and talked before his time."

Black Louisville was divided into three sections—East End, the California area, and West End, where the Clays lived. Like most of the families in the neighborhood, they were poor. The family car was always at least 10 years old with worn-out tires. The house always needed painting. The front porch sagged, and during rainy weather, water leaked through the roof and walls. Many of the children's clothes were secondhand. Once in a while, the Clays were able to afford a new shirt or a new pair of pants for Cassius and his younger brother, Rudy—but not often.

Odessa Grady Clay worked as a domestic when her sons were young, cleaning houses and caring for the children of well-to-do white families who lived on the other side of town. She earned four dollars a day. Odessa was a religious woman, and on Sundays, she and her two sons attended Mount Zion Baptist Church, where Cassius sang in the choir. She loved to talk, and she instilled in Cassius the values that he still follows—always treat people with kindness and never hate or be prejudiced.

His father, Cassius Marcellus Clay Sr., was a stern disciplinarian, and Cassius both loved and feared him. Cassius Sr. painted billboards and signs for a living. Almost every Baptist church in Louisville owned one of his murals, showing religious scenes. He taught Cassius and Rudy how to paint signs. But he never wanted his sons to follow in his footsteps. He wanted them to become doctors or lawyers. There wasn't much future for a black sign painter in Louisville in the 1940s and 1950s.

Like his wife Odessa, Cassius Sr. loved to talk and he was also a bit of a showman, bragging to friends, relatives, and strangers about his son's talents as a boxer, even before Cassius Jr. had his first fight. Cassius Sr. always told his son that he was "pretty as a picture," a phrase that Cassius later used to describe himself.

The Clays were a close-knit family but there was also a troubled side. Cassius Clay Sr. was arrested four times for reckless driving, twice for disorderly conduct, and twice for assault and battery. When he had too much to drink he became violent. Odessa Clay called the police several times seeking protection from her husband.

At that time, Louisville was segregated, with blacks living in separate neighborhoods from whites. Black people were allowed to sit only in the back rows of buses and movie theaters. Most stores and restaurants wouldn't serve blacks, not even a drink of water for a thirsty child. Black children and white children could not attend school together. And if Cassius was on the wrong side of town, people would call him "nigger" and demand that he leave. "When I was a kid in Kentucky," he recalled, "a Negro couldn't ride in the front of a bus or drink a cup of coffee where he wanted, or go to the movies anywhere he felt like it."

In the South when Clay was a boy, drinking fountains and public facilities were labeled "white only" and "colored only." Segregation was the law.

When Cassius was 12, his father bought him a brand new Schwinn bicycle for Christmas, at what was likely a great sacrifice to the Clay finances. Cassius proudly pedaled throughout the neighborhood. He rode with a friend one day to a large bazaar in town called the Louisville Home Show, held at the Columbia Auditorium. The two boys parked their bicycles outside. They looked at home furnishings and crafts and munched on free popcorn and candy. When they left the show, Cassius couldn't find his bicycle. It had been stolen.

A police officer and amateur boxing coach, Joe Martin, was teaching boxing in the basement of the auditorium, in the Columbia Boxing Gym. Someone suggested that Cassius report the bicycle theft to Martin. Cassius ran up to the police officer and told him angrily, "If I find the kid who stole my bike, I'll whip him!"

Martin replied, "If you plan to whip somebody, maybe you'd better come down [to the gym] and learn how."

Cassius almost forgot that his bicycle was missing when he looked around the gym. Boys were boxing each other and skipping rope. He could hear the rat-tat-tat of the speed bag and the hard punches to the heavy bag. The air smelled like perspiration and liniment. Joe Martin invited the excited Cassius to join his boxing club and sent him home with an application.

The bicycle, unfortunately, was never found. But a few days later, while he was changing channels on the television, Cassius noticed Joe Martin coaching amateur boxers on a show called *Tomorrow's Champions.* Cassius decided that he would join Martin's gym.

"I want to be a boxer," he told his mother. His parents thought that boxing would be better for Cassius than roaming the streets with his friends.

He weighed only 89 pounds and had never put on boxing gloves before. But he went to the gym every day. "He stood out because, I guess, he had more determination than most boys," Martin said, "and he had the speed to get him someplace." Cassius learned how to throw punches, how to hit the heavy bag and the speed bag, and how to jump rope.

He was thin and wiry but he made an impression, mastering punches like a professional. He spent almost all of his spare time in the gym. Confident and poised, he wasn't rattled when he was hit. His feet moved as quickly as his hands, and after a fight he would pretend to announce over the loudspeaker: "Ladies and gentlemen, introducing the new world champion . . . "

Heavyweight champions of Clay's boyhood: The legendary Joe Louis attempts a comeback against Rocky Marciano, 1951.

Six weeks after he first walked into Joe Martin's gym, Cassius was scheduled to appear on *Tomorrow's Champions*. He knocked on the doors of his neighbors' houses to tell them that he was going to fight on television. Often chased by the larger boys in the neighborhood, he would prove with this fight how tough he really was.

On the day of the show, he stepped into the ring against a boy from one of Louisville's white neighborhoods. A nervous Cassius punched and ducked and bobbed and weaved for three two-minute rounds. When the bell rang to signal the end of the fight and the judges' scorecards were added up, the winner was Cassius Clay!

He grew more confident after his victory and began to get recognition from friends and family. "He was a very happy little boy," his mother recalled. "When he was 12, he said he's going to be champion of the world."

Cassius and his friends were afraid of a bully who terrorized the children in the neighborhood—until the day Cassius challenged the bully to a fight at the high school gym. Cassius threw a few punches, and the bully ran home with a bloody nose. Cassius was now known as "the King."

Only a few things interested him besides boxing. He loved to shoot marbles, and he would sometimes wake up early in the morning to watch the horses train at Churchill Downs, a famous racetrack in Louisville. He loved the stables and the smell of the horses and their sleek, muscular bodies. He would race alongside them as they sped by during their practice runs.

He kept busy after school, training and traveling to boxing tournaments with Joe Martin's team of amateur fighters. "Kids used to throw rocks and stand under the street lights. But there wasn't nothing to do in the streets," he later said about his childhood. "I tried it a little bit but [there] wasn't nothing else to do but boxing."

The King did his roadwork every morning. "He was a very devoted kid," said Joe Martin. He would wake up at 4:00 A.M., run for two hours, go home to sleep again, and arrive at DuValle Junior High School at 9:00. Sometimes he and Rudy raced the bus for 20 blocks to school. The children on the bus laughed at them, but Cassius told people that he was running to get in fighting shape.

Cassius bragged that he was the toughest kid in Louisville. He ate a healthful diet. He never drank or smoked cigarettes. As a teenager, he dated a few girls, including Mildred Davis during his senior year in high school. She remembers that Cassius was the class clown—always goofing off in school, joking, and shadowboxing in the halls.

But around girls he was different—polite and shy. One day Cassius let Mildred wear a pendant—a little gold glove on gold chain. The pendant was part of his prize for winning the National Golden Gloves Championships in Chicago.

Cassius wasn't very attentive in class, and he didn't spend much time on homework. Instead he went to the gym. "I saw there was no future in getting a high school education or even a college education," Cassius later said. "There was no future because I knew too many that had [diplomas] and were laying around on the corner. A boxer has something to do every day."

Cassius graduated from Louisville's Central High School with a D-minus average—376th out of a class of 391. Some teachers thought Cassius shouldn't be allowed

Young Cassius Clay—ready to take on the world

to graduate because of his poor grades. But principal Atwood Wilson argued on Cassius's behalf: "Why, in one night, he'll make more money than the principal and all you teachers make in one year," Wilson said. "If every teacher here fails him, he's still not going to fail." On June 11, 1960, Cassius received his high school diploma to a standing ovation from his classmates. Now he would pursue his boxing career full-time.

"I started boxing because I thought this was the fastest way for a black person to make it in this country. I was not that bright in school. I couldn't be a football player or basketball player because you have to go to college and get all kinds of degrees and pass examinations," he said.

"A boxer can just go to the gym, jump around, turn professional, win a fight, get a break, and he is in the ring. If he's good enough he makes more money than ballplayers make all their lives."

First stop on the road to the top: the Olympic Games

CHAPTER THREE

STING LIKE
A BEE

YOUNG CASSIUS CLAY WAS BLESSED WITH FAST
feet and faster hands, and he learned quickly. He was the
first one to arrive at the gym and the last one to leave.
"When he first put on the gloves," Joe Martin recalled, "it
was easy to see that he had a natural flair for the sport. He
was quick and made pretty good moves for a kid with no
formal instruction."

By the time he was 18 years old, Cassius had won six
Kentucky Golden Gloves tournaments, two National
Golden Gloves Championships, and, in 1959 and 1960,
two National AAU (Amateur Athletic Union) titles. He
had won 100 out of 108 amateur fights and wanted to
turn professional.

But Joe Martin convinced him to try out for the United

States Olympic team instead. "In boxing, the Olympic champion is already good as the number one ranked pro," Martin explained. Cassius won an elimination tournament to earn a spot on the team.

The 1960 Olympics were held in Rome, Italy, and the enthusiastic and outgoing Cassius Clay became the most popular athlete at the Games. He waved and called hello to everyone he met, shaking hands, signing autographs, and sitting for interviews.

He was introduced to Floyd Patterson, the heavyweight champion and a former Olympic gold medalist. Cassius predicted that the two fighters would soon meet for the

The U.S. Olympic boxing team in Rome. Clay (far right) *competed as a light heavyweight.*

heavyweight title. "So long, Floyd, be seeing you—in about two years—when I whip you for your title," he told the unimpressed Patterson.

Cassius had not yet filled out as a heavyweight, which was 179 pounds and above in Olympic competition. He competed as a light heavyweight at 178 pounds and beat three opponents easily to qualify for the finals.

In the fight for the gold medal, he beat Zbigniew Pietrzykowski of Poland, a three-time European champion who had won a bronze medal at the previous Olympics. The referee held Cassius's hand up in victory. He waved the American flag and waved to the crowd.

After the fight, he didn't want to take off his gold medal, even at night. "I didn't sleep too good because I had to sleep on my back so the medal wouldn't cut me," he recalled. "But I didn't care. I was the Olympic champ." Back home, his father painted the cement steps to the front porch in red, white, and blue.

On the way back from Rome, Cassius stopped in New York City as part of the Olympic celebration. He visited Greenwich Village and Times Square. Many people had seen Cassius win the gold medal on television. Tourists recognized him and asked for his autograph. He introduced himself as "Cassius Clay, the great fighter."

He met Sugar Ray Robinson, then world welterweight and middleweight champion. At Robinson's restaurant in New York City, Cassius asked Sugar Ray to be his manager. But Robinson, still fighting himself, wasn't interested in working with the younger fighter.

Back in Louisville, the town turned out for a giant parade, and the returning hero waved to the crowds from the back of a pink Cadillac. "Boxing made me feel like somebody different," he said. "I always liked attention and publicity."

Although Cassius had represented the United States in the Olympics and had won the gold medal, he was still a black man. In many parts of the South, African Americans were denied the right to vote. They rode—by law—in the backs of buses, drank from water fountains for blacks only, attended all-black schools, and weren't allowed to stay in most hotels. Finding a well-paying job was difficult—in some small towns, impossible. Blacks were often called "niggers" and treated like second-class citizens.

A famous story says that in Louisville, the gold medal still hanging from his neck, Cassius and a friend stopped in a restaurant for a hamburger. But the owner of the restaurant wouldn't serve black people. "[Cassius] said, 'I'm the light heavyweight champion, the gold medal winner,'" recalled his brother, Rudy, "and they said 'I don't give a damn what you are, you can't get no food in here.'"

Outside the restaurant, a white motorcycle gang leader taunted Cassius and demanded his gold medal. A fight broke out. Afterward, Cassius became so disgusted with the way that he and other black people were treated in the United States that he threw his precious gold medal into the Ohio River—or so the story goes.

The story has been told again and again. Some people think the story was made up—or at least exaggerated over the years. One part of the story isn't fiction, though. Cassius was indeed turned away from many restaurants in his hometown and in other southern cities. After the Olympics, he began to speak publicly against racial discrimination in the United States.

Cassius had many offers to turn professional after the Olympics, and he selected the Louisville Sponsoring Group, an association of 11 wealthy, white businessmen as his management company. The company would choose Cassius's opponents, set up bouts, and negotiate contracts for radio and television broadcasts of his fights.

Cassius Sr. helped negotiate his son's contract with the Louisville Group. The young fighter would receive a $10,000 bonus for signing, a salary of $4,000 a year for two years, and $6,000 a year for the next four years. He would receive 50 percent of his prize money, or purses, and 50 percent of his earnings outside the ring (from public appearances). The Louisville Group would pay his training expenses and set aside money for him in a trust fund.

Cassius's immediate goals were to buy a house for his parents and a brand new red Cadillac for himself. The Louisville Group's first priority was to pair Cassius with a trainer who would polish his skills and teach him how to box as a professional.

He was first sent to train with former light heavyweight champion and heavyweight contender Archie Moore at Moore's training camp in California. But their personalities clashed. Moore, 47, was disciplined and quiet, in contrast to the outgoing Clay. So they parted. They were to meet later as opponents.

Cassius then teamed up with Angelo Dundee, the trainer of seven champions. "There was something special about him even then," said Dundee. "I smoothed Cassius out and put some snap in his punches." A young Clay disagreed: "Dundee gave me the jab. But the rest is me."

Cassius moved to Miami, Florida, where Dundee trained his fighters. Cassius lived in a one-room apartment in a rough neighborhood. He trained at Miami's Fifth Street Gym, on the second story, where the floor sagged and the windows were unwashed. The gym was decorated with fight posters and old photographs, and people paid 50 cents to watch the fighters work out.

Cassius enjoyed living on his own and visiting the clubs around Miami. He liked Fats Domino, Little Richard, Sam Cooke, Chubby Checker, and other black musicians of the day. But he tried to stay focused on his goals. "The hardest part of the training is the loneliness," he admitted in a quiet moment. "Here I am, just nineteen, surrounded by showgirls, whiskey and sissies, and nobody watching me. But it takes a mind to do right. I'd be plenty silly to give in to temptation now."

Just as in Louisville, Cassius was always the first one at the gym and the last one to leave. He would fight anyone. Angelo Dundee was impressed by his dedication and natural ability.

Professional fights range from 4 rounds for beginners' matches to 12 rounds for championship fights (15 rounds

Cassius liked to sing almost as much as he liked to talk.

when Cassius Clay began his career). Three judges award points to each fighter based on his performance. The man with the most points at the end of the match wins. This type of victory is called "winning by decision." The winner can also be determined early—if one opponent is knocked out (doesn't get up within 10 seconds after a fall) or if the referee stops the fight because one opponent is unable to continue defending himself.

In his professional debut, in October 1960, Cassius Clay launched his career by facing Tunney Hunsaker at the Louisville Convention Center. Hunsaker was not highly rated and was considered a safe opponent, someone Clay was likely to beat, because of his 17-8 record and his age—he was 29. Clay outdanced and outboxed Hunsaker, winning a six-round unanimous decision—all three judges gave Clay the highest score. He received $2,000 in prize money.

"I'd never dreamt a big man could move as fast as he did," said Hunsacker, whose eyes were swollen shut after the fight. "I pulled every trick I'd learned in the pro ranks, and it didn't bother him." Hunsaker predicted: "As soon as he's given the opportunity, he'll be world champion."

Clay won his next 14 bouts. And he started to attract national attention—giving interviews, reciting poetry, and making headlines. Reporters from newspapers, radio, and television became enamored of Clay—he was handsome and colorful—and he always gave them interesting quotes. "I'm so fast I can turn out the light and be in bed before it's dark," he declared.

He loved the camera and the camera loved him. Photographers admired his expressive face. Women fell for him one after another. But despite his outgoing personality, his rhymes, jokes, and boasts, Cassius had a quiet side. In private, when the reporters had left the room, he often became shy and thoughtful.

At the end of 1962, he faced his biggest test to date. Archie Moore, the former light heavyweight champion, who was now 49, was to be his challenger. Clay was 20 years old and favored to win, even though he had had only 15 professional fights. Moore had had more than 200.

The fight would be Clay's first against a big-name fighter. He sang this rhyme at press conferences before the fight:

When you come to the fight
Don't block the aisles and don't block the door
I'll say it again, I've said it before
Archie Moore will fall in four.

And another rhyme:

Archie's been living off the fat of the land
I'm here to give him his pension plan.

Clay stood 6 feet, 3 inches and weighed a trim 204 pounds. Moore, with a smaller frame, was overweight at 197. When the bell rang to begin the fight, Moore stood in his trademark crablike crouch, with his arms crossed to protect his jaw and his chin.

Clay kept punching and wore him down. In the fourth

round, Clay hit Moore with a right, and Moore lost his mouthpiece. Clay, with a combination of punches, sent Moore to the canvas. Moore managed to get up, only to be knocked down again. He got up again and went down for the third and final time. Clay knocked him out, as predicted, one minute and 35 seconds into the fourth round. Clay was too young, too fast, and too big for him. It was Moore's last fight.

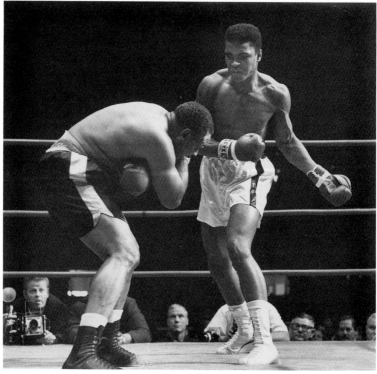

Archie Moore buckles under Clay's punches.

Seven of Clay's last eight fights had ended in the round that he had predicted. He became even more popular with the press and the fans. Early the next year, he fought Doug Jones.

"If Jones wants to mix, I'll end it in six," he predicted. He promoted himself on *The Tonight Show,* an unusual showcase for a fighter at the time. New York's Madison Square Garden was sold out for a professional fight for the first time in a decade.

But this matchup turned out to be one of the worst fights of Clay's career. It didn't end in six. After so much publicity, it was an unimpressive bout, with Jones performing at his best and the fight ending in a 10-round decision in favor of Clay. An unimpressed crowd threw trash, program books, bottles, and peanuts into the ring. "I sure underestimated Jones," Clay conceded.

Just after the fight, Clay met a man named Bundini Brown and added him to his staff without an official job title. Brown became a close friend who could motivate Clay, a cheerleader who could push him in training and through fights. Brown also helped Clay with his poetry. It was Brown who coined the phrase "Float like a butterfly, sting like a bee."

Clay rode around in his Cadillac, listening to music with his friends. "I'm not training too hard for this bum," he said of his next opponent, Henry Cooper. At the fight in London, held on June 18, 1963, he entered the ring in a red robe inscribed "Cassius the Greatest." Although he eventually knocked out the former British heavyweight champion, Clay was knocked down for the first time in his career. He was back on his feet quickly. "I am the greatest!" he shouted after the referee stopped the fight. His toughest test was to follow.

In his 20th professional bout, Clay challenged Sonny Liston for the heavyweight title. Today's heavyweight championship is split among several fighters, who hold titles awarded by different governing bodies—the World Boxing Council, the World Boxing Association, and the International Boxing Federation.

The heavyweight champion of the world when Cassius Clay began his career was THE heavyweight champion—the one and only heavyweight champion. The fight against Liston would give Clay the chance to prove that he was the greatest boxer in the world.

Sonny Liston, 220 pounds of solid muscle, rarely smiled or showed any expression in his face. With his fast left hook, he was considered unbeatable. He had turned pro in 1953, when he was 20, winning 34 bouts and losing just one before he met Floyd Patterson for the heavyweight title in 1962. He had knocked Patterson out in the first round to claim the championship.

For the heavyweight championship fight, to be held on February 25, 1964, Clay trained at the Fifth Street Gym. By now, he was a celebrity. Even the Beatles, in Miami Beach to begin a concert tour, stopped by and posed with him for photographs. The pictures showed Clay playfully pretending to box and to knock out the famous musicians.

The weigh-in before a fight is usually a quiet affair. But

at this one, held the day before the fight at the Miami Convention Center, Clay stormed around in a carefully rehearsed show, waving his hands wildly and shouting at Liston:

We're going to rumble!

Where's the ugly bear?

Float like a butterfly, sting like a bee!

Liston is nothing. I'm the greatest fighter who ever lived and I'm going to upset the world!

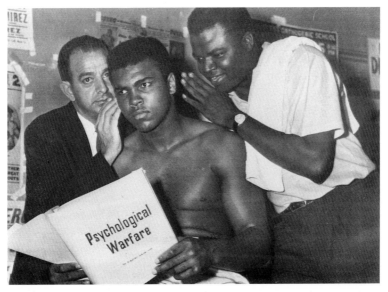

Angelo Dundee, Cassius Clay, and Bundini Brown say that they'll use "psychological warfare" against Sonny Liston.

The physician for the Miami Boxing Commission said that Clay was "emotionally unbalanced, scared to death and liable to crack up in the ring." Some reporters believed his diagnosis, others took Clay's performance for the act that it was. Headlines were written: "Cassius the Brashest," "The Louisville Lip," and "The Mighty Mouth."

"I wanted Liston to know that I was crazy," Clay said. "Who but a fool isn't scared of a crazy man?"

Clay was not expected to win. He entered the ring first, wearing a short, white, hooded robe that read "The Lip." When the fight began, Liston was slow and plodding. Clay was the opposite—fast with jabs, combinations, and

Cassius takes out the Beatles—Paul, John, Ringo, and George—with one blow.

quick footwork. He carried his hands low, leaning back from punches and moving off the ropes.

Liston's punches kept missing, and in the third round, Clay cut him on the left side of his face. Liston had fought 40 times before this matchup, and he had never once been cut.

Liston returned to his corner, and his staff treated the cut with an anticoagulant, medication that would stop the bleeding. Somehow, either this liquid or a liniment

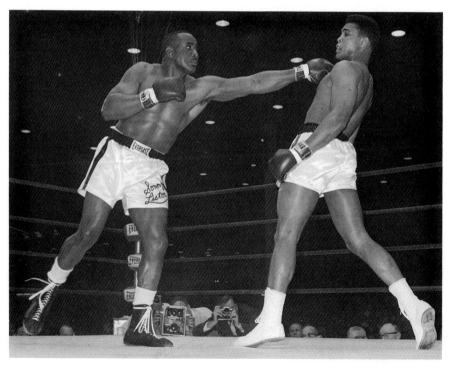

Liston can't hit the moving target.

used on Liston's shoulder ended up on his boxing gloves. In the next round, when Liston pushed his gloves into Clay's face, the medication got into Clay's eyes, burning them and nearly blinding him.

Clay tried to wipe the substance out of his eyes with his gloves. He swung wildly and instinctively. After the end of the round he shouted to Angelo Dundee, "Cut my gloves off! I can't see! We're going home."

Dundee refused, flushing his fighter's eyes with water and pushing him off his stool. Liston was still a blur, and Clay blindly ducked out of the way of his punches. When his eyes finally cleared in the sixth round, Clay began pushing Liston's head back with his fists. Bundini Brown shouted encouragement from outside of the ring.

Liston was exhausted and battered. Before the bell rang for the start of the seventh round, he shook his head wearily and slumped on his stool. He quit, too tired to continue.

Cassius Clay was the new heavyweight champion. "I am king!" he shouted. "I am the greatest! I shook up the world!"

At the press conference afterward, he silenced the crowd of reporters and demanded: "Who's the greatest?"

"I give you one more chance. . . . Who's the greatest?"

"You are," the crowd responded.

"Alright," he said, satisfied.

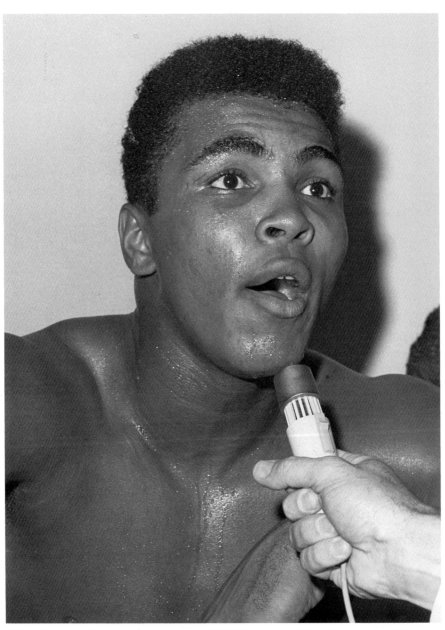

Clay would soon become more famous for his remarks outside of the boxing ring than for his skills inside it.

CHAPTER FOUR

DON'T CALL
ME CASSIUS

CASSIUS CLAY'S BOXING HERITAGE, AS WELL AS that of every other black fighter, followed the heavy-weight champions Jack Johnson and Joe Louis. Johnson, standing 6 feet, 1 inch and weighing 195 pounds, was born John Arthur Johnson in 1878 in Galveston, Texas. He was known for his fast left and his excellent defense. In 1908, he fought for the heavyweight title, beating Tommy Burns in Sydney, Australia. Johnson's reign was a long one, lasting seven years.

Joe Louis gained a large following through radio broad-casts of his fights. With excellent power in each hand, he was called invincible. He turned pro in 1934 and fought for the heavyweight title in 1937, knocking out James Braddock in the eighth round to become the champion.

Louis defended his title 25 times, losing only three bouts in his career.

Each fighter was a product of his times. When Jack Johnson was champion, American society was strictly segregated, and most whites treated blacks with hostility. There were many black fighters then, but it was hard for them to prove their talents because most white boxers refused to fight a black man. Johnson enraged many whites by showing that blacks could be superior athletes.

Jack Johnson

Joe Louis

Joe Louis was not a vocal supporter of rights for black people. He served in a segregated army unit during World War II and never questioned racial discrimination in the military or in American society. But he was held up as a role model for black youngsters when the civil rights movement was just beginning.

By the time Cassius Clay came along, African Americans had begun to stand up for their rights. White Americans were opening up to change, were willing to be pushed a little, and Clay pushed them. He demanded to be heard, to be treated with dignity and given equal rights.

The late 1950s and early 1960s were a time of profound change in the United States. The civil rights movement gathered strength in 1955, when Rosa Parks refused to give her seat to a white man on a bus in Montgomery, Alabama. By law, blacks in Montgomery had to sit in the rear sections of city buses. Black passengers had to give up their seats to white passengers if a bus was full.

Park's action ignited a citywide bus boycott. Black citizens refused to support a bus system that denied them equal treatment. Finally, more than a year after the boycott began, seating restrictions were dropped on Montgomery buses.

More protests followed. In February 1960, four black students sat down at a Woolworth's "whites-only" lunch counter in Greensboro, North Carolina. They asked to be served and refused to leave when they weren't. They returned the next day with two dozen friends. They brought twice as many people the following day, and by the fifth day, more than 300 black people had gathered at the lunch counter, claiming their right to be served.

Led by Dr. Martin Luther King Jr., blacks "sat-in" at other segregated restaurants and held protests throughout the South. Some protesters were beaten, some were killed. At a civil rights march in Birmingham, Alabama, black men, women, and children and white sympathizers were attacked with cattle prods, water hoses, and police dogs. Throughout the South, black men were lynched, crosses were burned in front of black homes, and black churches were firebombed.

Many black athletes chose to be silent on civil rights. They focused on their sports, not on politics. But Cassius Clay would not be silent. "Here I am, the heavyweight champion of the world," he said. "I have brought honor to my country, and I can't get a cup of coffee in downtown Louisville because I'm black."

A sit-in at a lunch counter in Arkansas, early 1960s

"America is supposed to mean freedom, isn't it?" he said on another occasion. "What [the] white man don't understand is that it's the hurtin'est thing in the world to be black and live in a ghetto. You prove you're a man by throwing bricks. If you're successful and intelligent they don't respect you—they roll over you."

To many blacks, Cassius Clay was a hero. To some whites, he was threatening. "Here comes Cassius," said black leader Malcolm X, "the exact contrast of everything that was representative of the Negro image. He said he was the greatest, all the odds were against him, he upset the oddsmakers, he won, he became the champion. They [white people] knew as soon as [black] people began identifying with Cassius and the kind of image he was creating, they were going to have trouble out of these Negroes because they'd have Negroes walking around the street saying 'I'm the greatest.'"

Unknown to most people, Clay had been attending meetings of the Nation of Islam, a black religious group founded in the United States in 1930. Nation of Islam members practice a version of the Muslim (Islamic) religion. They pray to Allah.

During the 1960s, Nation of Islam leaders argued that blacks and whites should remain separate. They believed that the black population should form a separate nation within the United States. Many Nation of Islam members called white people "the devil." At a time when civil rights leaders were working to end segregation in schools, restaurants, buses, hotels, and neighborhoods, the Nation of Islam angered many people within the black as well as the white community.

At the Olympics in 1960, Cassius had read a copy of the Nation of Islam newspaper, *Muhammad Speaks.* A year later, a devoted follower of Elijah Muhammad, the head of the Nation of Islam, encouraged Cassius to attend the group's meetings.

Cassius began reading *Muhammad Speaks* regularly. Malcolm X, one of the most prominent members of the

In New York City, Cassius, his brother Rudy, and Malcolm X meet with S. O. Abedo, Nigeria's ambassador to the United Nations.

Nation of Islam, visited him often at the Fifth Street Gym.
For three years before the fight with Sonny Liston, Cassius
and his brother Rudy snuck into Nation of Islam meetings
at a Muslim temple in Miami. "I didn't want people to
know that I was there," he said. "I was afraid, if they
knew, that I wouldn't be allowed to fight for the title."

Reporters suspected that Clay had joined the Nation of
Islam. But it wasn't until a press conference after the title
fight with Liston that he formally announced his mem-
bership in the group.

"People brand us a hate group," he said. "They say we
want to take over the country. They say we're Communists. That is not true. Followers of Allah are the sweetest
people in the world. . . . All they want to do is live in
peace. . . . You can't condemn a man for wanting peace."

Cassius also said that he had changed his name to
Muhammad Ali, which means "someone who is worthy
of praise." Ali's great-grandfather, a slave, had taken the
name Clay from his owner. Ali told reporters: "Don't call
me by my slave name no more."

"I chose to be a Muslim," he continued. "I chose to be a
follower of Elijah Muhammad because he was the only
one offering definite plans which helped my people."

Many members of the press and the public felt that Ali
had tarnished his Olympic gold medal by his involvement
with the Nation of Islam. "I don't have to be what you
want me to be," he retorted. "I'm free to be who I want."

The Nation of Islam began to exert a great deal of influence over Muhammad Ali's life and career. Shortly after

In the gym, Ali stayed focused.

the announcement of Ali's conversion to Islam, Herbert Muhammad, the son of Elijah Muhammad, became Ali's new manager. Eventually, all ties with the Louisville Sponsoring Group were severed.

Bundini Brown refused to join the Nation of Islam, as did Ali's parents. "Even though I'm not a Muslim," Brown said, "I respect him for being one because he loves it and that's what makes him happy." Ali's mother held a more skeptical view of the Muslims. "There's only one reason why they don't throw him out," she said angrily. "They want him for his money and his popularity."

Although Elijah Muhammad taught that blacks were the superior race and that whites were the devil, Ali held a more moderate view of race relations. He embraced everyone. "Hearts and souls have no color," he said.

After the Liston fight, Ali traveled around the world. He spent a month in Africa—in Ghana, Nigeria, and Egypt—meeting the public and visiting heads of state. Dressed in a white shirt and a slim tie—and sometimes the traditional dress of his host countries—he waved to the crowds who clustered around him and ran after him.

When Ali returned to the United States, Herbert Muhammad introduced him to 23-year-old Sonji Roi from Chicago. Ali fell in love with her. "I met Muhammad Ali on a Wednesday in the afternoon and I never left him," she said. "He asked me to marry him five minutes [later]." In August 1964, just 41 days after they met, Muhammad Ali and Sonji Roi were married in Gary, Indiana.

"Cassius KO'd by Cupid" read one headline. There was

no time for a honeymoon. Ali had to return to Florida to train for his next fight.

Roi was an unusual choice for Ali because she didn't fit the Muslim mold. Muslim women were supposed to dress modestly—with veils and long dresses that reached the floor. Roi worked in nightclubs and sometimes modeled for photographers. She wore makeup, smoked cigarettes, and refused to wear the Muslim dress. Many of Ali's friends didn't like her.

Sonji and Muhammad, August 1964

Sonji tried to follow the Islamic practices for a while. But she questioned the Muslims. She didn't like the influence they had over her husband's life. The marriage was shaky from the start.

Ali was scheduled to meet Sonny Liston for a second fight, this time in Lewiston, Maine, in May 1965. The former champion was now the challenger. As soon as the fight began, Ali took the lead. Because he was so fast, he made Liston look even slower. He moved his upper body quickly, causing Liston to miss with his punches.

Proving that his early victory was no fluke, Ali knocked out Liston in the first round with a short right

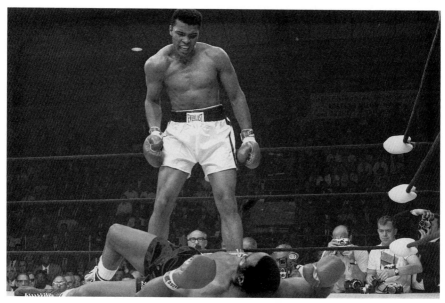

Ali yells at Liston to stand up and keep fighting.

punch. Some spectators did not see the punch, but it hit Liston square on the temple. Liston crumbled and rolled over. He tried to get up but he fell down again.

Ali taunted him. "Get up! Get up, you yellow bum!" he shouted at the prone Liston. Liston staggered to his feet, but it was too late. The referee had stopped the fight.

The fight was controversial. People who hadn't seen the final punch insisted that the outcome had been arranged in advance. "Fix! Fix!" they shouted. But films of the fight showed that Liston was hit hard.

Ali had proved again that he was heavyweight champion of the world. "I'm the World Champion but I don't feel any different than that fan over there," he said. "I'll still walk in the ghettos, answer questions, and kiss babies. I'll never forget my people."

He was called the people's champion. True to his word, he often took walks through inner-city neighborhoods and met with fans. If he saw a homeless man, he might hand him a hundred-dollar bill or buy him a meal or a suit of clothes. Ali didn't like to fly on airplanes. When his schedule was tight, he had no choice but to travel by plane. But whenever possible, he and his staff went from fight to fight in a large bus. The words "Cassius Clay Enterprises" and "World's Most Colorful Fighter" were painted on the side of the bus. Wherever the bus stopped, people crowded around to meet Ali.

He rarely turned down an interview request—even high school newspaper reporters were welcome to sit and ask him questions. The ABC-TV sportscaster Howard

Ali turned boxing into show business. Here, he kids with performer Sammy Davis Jr.

Cosell was Ali's most famous interviewer. Cosell often played the "straight man" to Ali. He pretended to be serious while Ali told joke after joke. Fans loved their entertaining routine.

But Ali was not universally praised. Some reporters criticized Ali for using his fame to promote his religious beliefs. Many people in the media and the boxing community refused to use Ali's new name and continued to call him Cassius Clay.

Some people thought Ali was too outspoken. They didn't like the way he insulted his opponents, and many people cheered against him. Other people thought that Ali's rhymes and remarks were just a method of generating publicity. Indeed, Ali understood the show-business element of boxing, and he dominated the sports pages of newspapers. "It's hard to be humble when you're as great as I am," he said.

"I'm pretty as a picture," the champ often said.

Six months after he beat Liston for a second time, Ali defended his title against Floyd Patterson, former heavyweight champion, in Las Vegas, Nevada. Patterson, shy and quiet, had grown up in the Bedford-Stuyvesant section of Brooklyn, New York. In 1956, at age 21, he had knocked out Archie Moore in five rounds to become the heavyweight champion.

By the time Patterson met Ali, he had lost his title to Sonny Liston and was hoping to regain it. Patterson was 30 years old, Ali just 23. Ali didn't like Patterson, who insisted on calling him Cassius Clay. Patterson denounced the Muslims and called the Nation of Islam a menace to the United States.

Floyd Patterson is in trouble.

In return Ali called Patterson "a white man's Negro" and said he was "scared like a rabbit." Ali brought Patterson carrots before the fight. "I am going to punish him," Ali warned. "I am going to beat him so bad that he'll need a shoehorn to get his hat on."

The crowd in Las Vegas included baseball star Joe DiMaggio, singer Frank Sinatra, and actor James Garner. At the sound of the bell, Ali didn't take Patterson seriously. He didn't throw a single punch in the first round.

In the second round, Ali took control of the fight. It seemed as though he could knock out Patterson at any time. He was unmerciful, dominating the bout at a fast pace and throwing jab after jab. He pounded Patterson so badly that the referee stopped the fight in the 12th round.

Ali successfully defended his title seven times through 1966 and 1967, beating opponents George Chuvalo and Ernie Terrell by decision and knocking out all the others—Zora Folley, Henry Cooper, Brian London, Karl Mildenberger, and Cleveland Williams. Ali seemed unbeatable. Then his boxing career was halted.

With Howard Cosell looking on, Ali reports to a U.S. Army induction center in Houston.

CHAPTER FIVE

A DIFFERENT FIGHT

PRESIDENT LYNDON JOHNSON SIGNED SEVERAL important pieces of civil rights legislation in the 1960s: the Voting Rights Act of 1965 and the Civil Rights Acts of 1964 and 1968. But the struggle for racial equality was not over. And the turbulence in American society continued.

Johnson began bombing North Vietnam in 1965 to back the South Vietnamese government against the Communists of the North. By the end of 1967, the United States had dropped more than a half million tons of bombs on Vietnam. By late 1969, about 550,000 American troops were stationed in Vietnam, and nearly 40,000 had been killed.

Many Americans, particularly college students, opposed the war in Vietnam. In October 1967, 50,000 young people marched in Washington, D.C., to protest the war.

Some young men refused to register for the military draft. Others returned their draft cards to the government or burned the cards in protest. More than 10,000 young men evaded the draft by fleeing the country, usually going to Canada. Other men served four to five years in prison for draft evasion.

Muhammad Ali held the draft status of 1-Y, which meant that he was considered unfit for military service. His devotion to boxing had taken him away from his studies in junior high and high school, and he had scored low on army intelligence tests, particularly in the math section. His IQ (Intelligence Quotient) was listed as 78. "I only said I was the greatest," he reminded people, "I never said I was the smartest."

> I'M NOT BURNING MY DRAFT CARD. . . . IF I LOSE, I'M JUST GOING TO JAIL.

The public was not satisfied. Many people thought that Ali was lying about his intelligence. They wanted to know how someone who wrote poetry and captivated the media could be mentally unfit for the military.

Congressman Mendel Rivers of South Carolina said: "Clay's deferment [exemption] is an insult to every mother's son serving in Vietnam. Here he is, smart enough to finish high school, write his kind of poetry, promote himself all over the world, make a million a year, drive around in red Cadillacs—and they say he's too dumb to tote a gun. Who's dumb enough to believe that?"

New regulations lowered the intelligence requirements for army service in February 1966. Ali was reclassified as

1-A, which meant that he was eligible to be drafted into the army.

At first he didn't pay much attention to the Vietnam conflict. But as the controversy surrounding his draft status increased, he began to voice opposition to the war. He believed that African Americans had a more pressing battle to fight at home.

"I don't have nothing against them Viet Cong [the North Vietnamese]," he told reporters. "They never called me nigger. If I have to die I'll die fighting for freedom here." He also recited a rhyme:

> Keep asking me, no matter how long
> On the war in Vietnam, I sing this song
> I ain't got no quarrel with the Viet Cong.

Ali applied for conscientious objector status, claiming that his religious beliefs prevented him from serving in the military. The Nation of Islam preached peace, he explained. The group also considered itself to be a separate nation, and so refused to take part in a war for the United States.

Ali was denied an exemption and was called up for induction into the U.S. Army in April 1967. The army offered him a compromise: he wouldn't be placed in combat. He would be part of Special Services, the unit that entertained the troops. He could visit with troops and box in exhibition matches instead of fighting as a soldier.

Many people in the boxing community encouraged Ali to take the army's offer. They didn't want him to risk his career and his popularity by defying the U.S. Army. The penalty for draft evasion was harsh—typically five years in prison and a $5,000 fine.

Ali arrived at the U.S. Armed Forces Examining and Entrance Station in Houston on April 28, 1967, at 8:00 A.M.

Ali, here attending a Muslim convention in Chicago, requested exemption from the army on religious grounds.

He was one of 26 draftees called to the station for induction that day. Crowds of antiwar demonstrators chanted outside the building on Ali's behalf. Reporters waited to find out whether or not he would become a soldier.

Inside, Ali and the other young men filled out forms and took physical exams. At about 1:00 P.M., they reported to a ceremony room, where an officer read the draftees' names from an alphabetical list. When a man heard his name, he was supposed to step forward. With that gesture, he was officially inducted into the U.S. military. Each man stepped forward as his name was called. Then it was Ali's turn.

"Cassius Marcellus Clay," the officer said.

Ali didn't move.

The officer said a second time: "Cassius Marcellus Clay." Ali looked straight ahead.

This time, he was led from the room. A lieutenant formally notified Ali of the punishment for draft evasion. He would be given one last chance to step forward when his name was called.

"Cassius Marcellus Clay," the officer said a third time. Ali did not move. In a written statement he explained that he was a Muslim minister. He believed that he should be exempt from military service as were other clergymen. Again his request was denied.

Outside the building, the station's commanding officer told the media: "Ladies and gentlemen, Cassius Clay has just refused to be inducted into the United States Armed Forces." The news spread immediately. Ali would be

Ali addresses a Nation of Islam meeting in Houston.

prosecuted for draft evasion. In a four-page statement pre-
pared ahead of time, Ali explained: "I find I cannot be
true to my belief in my religion in accepting such a call."

Criticism was widespread. Parents of young men serving in Vietnam called Ali a traitor to the United States.
Former heavyweight champion Joe Louis, who had en-
listed in the army during World War II, commented, "I
think he should fight for his country." Baseball legend
Jackie Robinson, the first man to integrate major-league

baseball, agreed. He said, "I think he's hurting the morale of a lot of young Negro soldiers over in Vietnam and the tragedy to me is that Cassius has made millions of dollars off of the American public. Now he's not willing to show his appreciation to a country that's giving him a fantastic opportunity."

Milton Gross of the *New York Post* wrote that "as a man, he cannot compare to some of the kids slogging through the rice paddies [of Vietnam] where the names are stranger than Muhammad Ali." The Kentucky State Legislature condemned Ali, saying that "his attitude brings discredit to all loyal Kentuckians and to the names of thousands who gave their lives for this country during his lifetime." Former light heavyweight champion Billy Conn called him "a disgrace to the boxing profession."

Others were more supportive. "No matter what you think of Muhammad Ali's religion," preached Martin Luther King Jr. from his pulpit, "you certainly have to admire his courage."

A group of prominent black athletes called Ali to a meeting in Cleveland. Football star Jim Brown, basketball greats Bill Russell and Lew Alcindor (later know as Kareem Abdul-Jabbar), and others talked with Ali about his stance against the war. After the meeting, the athletes announced their support for his decision.

Before the case against Ali could be heard in court, the World Boxing Association and the New York State Athletic Commission stripped him of the heavyweight title and revoked his boxing license. There was no hearing by the commission. The front page of the *New York Times* carried the headline: "Clay Refuses Army Oath; Stripped of Boxing Crown."

"We can take a fighter's title for any acts which we consider not conducive to the best interests of boxing," explained Edwin B. Dooley, the chairman of the New York State Athletic Commission. Every other state followed New York's lead. "It was an outrage, an absolute disgrace," said Howard Cosell about the decision to revoke Ali's license. "Due process of law hadn't even begun."

MY GHOST WILL HAUNT ALL THE ARENAS.

Ali's trial began on June 19, 1967. Mobs of people showed up in the courtroom to support him. "I'm not burning my draft card," he said solemnly, dressed in a dark suit and tie. "I still have it. I'm going to be a man and fight it legally. If I lose, I'm just going to jail."

The judge found Ali guilty of draft evasion and gave him the maximum sentence: a fine of $10,000 and five years in jail. Ali's attorneys immediately appealed the court's decision, which meant that he didn't have to go to jail. But his license was still revoked, so he couldn't earn a living by boxing. His passport was canceled, so he wasn't able to fight overseas.

People still wanted to see Ali. But instead of watching him fight, they would hear him speak. He began to travel around the country, speaking on college campuses, defending his position on the draft, explaining the Nation of Islam philosophy, and talking about his fights. He spoke at Yale, Harvard, Princeton, Columbia, Howard (an all-black college in Washington, D.C.), and dozens of other campuses. Hundreds of students gathered on steps and leaned out of windows to listen to him.

Ali always started his speeches by saying that he was still the heavyweight champion of the world. "Everybody knows I'm the champion," he said. "My ghost will haunt all the arenas. I'll be there, wearing a sheet and whispering 'Ali-e-e-e! Ali-e-e-e!'" Occasionally a heckler would call from the audience: "Nigger!" or "Draft dodger!" The Federal Bureau of Investigation, considering Ali a threat to the United States, monitored his speeches.

Ali had lost his title and his career. But he cared more about his personal convictions than about his fame or fortune. "Damn the money. Damn the heavyweight championship. I will die before I sell out my people for the white man's money," he said in one speech. "The wealth of America and the friendship of all the people who support the war would be nothing if I'm not content internally and if I'm not in accord with the will of the Almighty Allah."

Banished from boxing, Ali took his message to young people all over the United States.

Peoples Champion

The EARLY TWENTIES ARE VITAL YEARS IN A fighter's career. But now Muhammad Ali was not a fighter. Instead he was a folk hero and a spokesman for social change. People who had never thought about the war in Vietnam suddenly paid attention to it.

Ali traveled from campus to campus in his bus. When he did not have a speaking engagement, he appeared on game shows and talk shows. "I've turned down millions to keep from selling out my people," he said on one TV show. At age 24, he had left behind his title, million-dollar purses, and all the perks given to the heavyweight champion. He told reporters in March 1967 that he had sacrificed nearly $9 million in advertisements, film deals, and record contracts for his beliefs.

He still made money from his fame—although far less than he would have made as a fighter. He received a $200,000 advance for his autobiography, *The Greatest: My Own Story,* coauthored by Richard Durham. He endorsed products and opened a chain of fast-food restaurants called Champburgers, which quickly folded. He worked with a group of filmmakers on *A/K/A Cassius Clay,* a documentary about his career.

He even appeared in the title role of an off-Broadway musical called *Buck White.* He was almost unrecognizable in a large Afro wig, a mustache, and a beard. Not a bad singer, he drew good reviews. "The show was bad, but I was great," he stated.

By this time, Ali and Sonji Roi had divorced. She hadn't followed the traditional Muslim practices, he charged in his divorce papers. Sonji blamed the Muslims for the failed marriage. "They wanted to control his entire life," she said. "I wasn't going to take on all the Muslims." The marriage ended bitterly.

Ali began to date different women. Many women were interested in the handsome fighter. But he preferred a woman who shared his faith. Belinda Boyd had been raised as a Muslim. She was soft-spoken and followed the Islamic customs. Belinda first met Muhammad in 1961 at a Muslim school in Chicago, where she was a young student and he was the visiting Olympic champion. The couple met again a few years later at a Nation of Islam convention and soon began to date.

"'You're gonna be my wife,'" she said he told her.

Second wife Belinda was a member of the Nation of Islam.

"He didn't ask me, he told me." On August 17, 1967, Muhammad and 17-year-old Belinda wed in Chicago. She joined him on his lecture tour of college campuses. Ten months later, their first daughter, Maryum Ali, was born.

In 1968 the World Boxing Association organized an eight-man elimination tournament to find Ali's successor. In the last round of the tournament, Jimmy Ellis fought Jerry Quarry for the heavyweight title, now considered vacant. Ellis won by a close decision. He defended his title against Joe Frazier in 1970 and was stopped in the fifth round.

Meanwhile, Howard Cosell and a handful of journalists and politicians led a movement to help Ali regain his boxing license. In September 1970, a federal court in New York ruled that the recall of Ali's license had been arbitrary and unreasonable. Georgia state senator Leroy Johnson helped arrange a bout for Ali in Atlanta.

The fight was scheduled for October 1970 against Jerry Quarry, a strong puncher. Some people felt that Ali shouldn't be allowed to fight. Both fighters received death threats. Ali received a package with a dead black dog and a note that read: "We know how to handle draft-dodging dogs in Georgia. Stay out of Atlanta."

But the fight was on. The crowd was filled with celebrities: actors Bill Cosby and Sidney Poitier, civil rights leader Jesse Jackson, and Martin Luther King's widow, Coretta Scott King. Limousines double-parked outside the arena, women wore furs and pearls, and men dressed in tuxedos.

Three and a half years after he had been expelled from boxing, Ali returned to the ring. He was 28 years old, the best years of his career gone. He was not the same Ali of 1967. He could no longer dance for 15 rounds, his movements were not as graceful, and he had lost some of his quickness. But he was talented enough to find a different way to fight.

Training in early 1970

He came out throwing punches and opened up a large cut over Quarry's eye in the third round. The referee stopped the fight. An annoyed Quarry did not want to stop fighting.

The crowd went wild. Ali was back. Two months later, he fought tough Oscar Bonavena in Madison Square Garden, knocking him down three times in the 15th round before finally knocking him out.

Ali's next fight would be against Joe Frazier, now recognized as the undisputed world champion. Frazier had turned pro in 1965. He had had 23 knockouts in 26 fights and was undefeated.

Ali weighed 215, Frazier 205. Standing 5 feet, 11 inches, Frazier was 4 inches shorter than Ali, and he was two years younger. He was a powerful fighter, a brawler who pummeled his opponents. His best weapon was his left hook, and he had a powerful right. He crouched and bore in relentlessly in the ring, less concerned with style than with effectiveness.

Ali, in contrast, was a smooth stylist who could outpunch his opponents with blows that seemed to come from everywhere. He held his hands low and moved quickly, leaning away from punches instead of stepping away.

The two fighters were opposites in personality, too. Ali loved the media, loved talking to reporters and being the center of attention. He called Frazier dumb, an "Uncle Tom" (a black man who acts subservient to whites) and a gorilla in a calculated plan of ridicule.

"Joe has always been a little slow in making out

Joe Frazier, shown here with trainer Eddie Futch, won the heavyweight title in 1970.

whether or not I'm serious or putting him on," Ali said. "He's not sure whether he is in on the joke or the joke is on him." Ali picked on Frazier's muddy South Carolina drawl, his grammar, vocabulary, and intelligence. "Joe Frazier is too ugly to be champ. Joe Frazier is too dumb to be champ," he said.

"Frazier's no real champion," he continued. "Anybody black who thinks Frazier can whup me is an Uncle Tom. Everybody who's black wants me to keep winning."

"I am the greatest!" Ali shouted to the microphones. "Invincible. Beautiful."

Frazier and Ali exchange insults as Howard Cosell (far left) *eggs the fighters on.*

Frazier, quiet and brooding, was businesslike and focused on the fight, not on the show. He fought for the sport of it and to support his wife and children. "This is just another man, another fight, another payday," he said beforehand.

"It ain't gonna be easy," Frazier said. "He's good and I'm good and that's what fights should be about." Angered by Ali's insults, he insisted on calling him Cassius Clay. "If I pass him in the desert and he's thirsting," Frazier warned, "I'll drive right by."

They were to meet on March 8, 1971, at Madison Square Garden. Each fighter would earn $2.5 million. But only one would be the heavyweight champion of the world. Ali was an 8 to 5 favorite with the oddsmakers. A month before the fight, all the tickets had been sold.

On the night of the fight, blocks and blocks of streets around Madison Square Garden were closed off. The fight was the biggest ever held in New York City. The crowd included celebrities such as Diana Ross and Frank Sinatra.

Ali played to the crowd, talking to Frazier and taking the first five rounds lightly. He looked like the Ali of old at times—moving, shuffling, ducking, and throwing sharp punches.

Frazier, with pressure and determination, threw punches with both hands to Ali's body, trying to weaken him. He bore in stubbornly, throwing hard punches that landed everywhere and digging his fists into Ali's ribs. Ali wasn't as fast as he had once been, his legs were slower, and he was slower to move out of the way. He

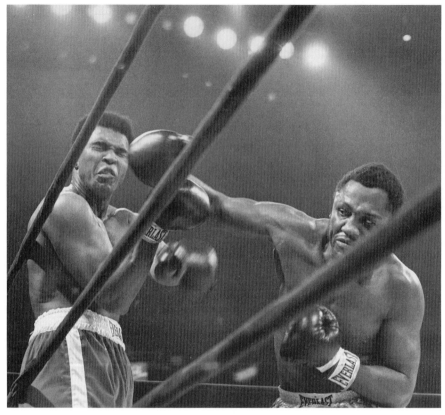

Frazier connects with a right to Ali's face.

absorbed more tough punches than he had in any previous fight. His body became red.

Frazier was taking a beating, too. His lip started bleeding and his face swelled up. In the 11th round, Frazier threw a left hook that wobbled the tired Ali, hurting him more than he'd ever been hurt in his career.

The next four rounds were just as brutal. In the 15th and final round, Frazier summoned up everything he had. He threw a massive left hook that landed on the tip of Ali's chin. Ali fell on his back with his feet up in the air, rolled over on his side, and then got up at the count of six.

Frazier won the fight by a unanimous decision. "I've been always handing [others] defeat," said Ali afterward. "Now I'm defeated." Both fighters were exhausted, both of their faces bruised, swollen, and misshapen. They both were taken to the hospital after the fight. It was Ali's first loss.

"The night of our first big fight," Frazier recalled, "Ali tried to hold a whole conversation with me in the ring. He was actually trying to talk me out of the fight. He kept telling me, 'I'm God,' and I told him, 'Oh, yeah? Well, God, you're in the wrong place 'cause God is gonna get his ass whipped tonight!'"

On the comeback trail

THE COMEBACK

"WHAT HURT MOST," SAID ALI AFTER THE LOSS TO Frazier, "wasn't the money that losing cost me. It wasn't the punches I took. It was knowing that my title was gone."

By this time, the draft evasion case against Ali had reached the U.S. Supreme Court. In June 1971, the Court reversed Ali's conviction by an 8-0 vote, ruling that his claim for conscientious objector status had been valid. All criminal charges against him were dropped.

With his legal struggles finally behind him, Ali began his comeback in the ring, rounding out the year with more fights. He beat Jimmy Ellis in Houston in his 32nd fight, won a decision over Buster Mathis, and knocked out a West German fighter named Jurgen Blin in the seventh round.

He met three former opponents the following year. George Chuvalo lost again, just as he had six years earlier. Jerry Quarry thought he had a chance to beat Ali, but he was mistaken, losing this time in the seventh round. Thirty-seven-year-old Floyd Patterson, still considering himself a contender, met Ali for a second time and also lasted to the seventh round. In Ali's last fight of 1972, he knocked out former light heavyweight champion Bob Foster, who weighed 41 pounds less, in the eighth round.

In 1972 Ali opened a training camp at Deer Lake in northwestern Pennsylvania. Boulders on the property were stenciled with names of fighters, with the centerpiece a 40-ton boulder representing Joe Louis. Ali built a gym, a dining hall, and cabins for sparring partners and guests. He hired his own cook and a large staff. Ali and his team ate at one large, round table. Water came from a well. "All, cold, natural, clear well water," he exclaimed. "Can't get this in the city."

Ali's entourage was a large one—often as many as 50 people surrounded him. His group of friends, staff, and followers included Bundini Brown, Angelo Dundee, Herbert Muhammad, photographer Howard Bingham who took thousands of pictures of the champ, and brother Rudy, now named Rahaman. Ali was rarely alone.

The door at Deer Lake was always open—fans, reporters, and the public were welcome. At first the neighbors in rural Pennsylvania were suspicious of Ali's camp. But neighbors sooned learned they were just as welcome as anyone. People came from miles around to watch Ali

Belinda Ali

train. He signed autographs and posed for pictures. In the evening, he did magic tricks to entertain the visitors.

When he wasn't training or traveling, Ali lived in a 16-room mansion in Chicago with Belinda and their children. In addition to Maryum, Muhammad and Belinda now had twin girls named Rasheeda and Jamillah, born in 1970. A boy, Muhammad Jr., was born in 1972. Sometimes, the whole family stayed at Deer Lake.

"Muhammad absolutely loved the children," Belinda recalled, "but he didn't have the patience to spend full-time with them." He was usually away from home, training or fighting.

Maryum Ali didn't like to watch her father's fights. She was afraid he would get hurt. Even when Ali was at home with the family, Maryum remembers, reporters, staff, and visitors were constantly streaming in and out of the house. "There weren't enough of those times when we were a family unit alone," she says.

In February 1973, Ali won a decision over Joe Bugner, his 10th win in a row since the fight with Frazier. He

The boulders at the Deer Lake honored famous fighters. Muhammad Ali and his daughters Maryum (foreground), Jamillah, and Rasheeda (behind her father) stroll by the monument to Sonny Liston.

came into the ring wearing a long robe decorated with jewels, a gift from his friend Elvis Presley. The words "People's Champion" were inscribed on the back.

One month later, he faced Ken Norton in San Diego. Norton, a former Marine and a former sparring partner of Joe Frazier's, was not considered much of an opponent, even though he was a well-conditioned fighter with a decent jab. An overconfident Ali took Norton lightly.

Norton was coached by Frazier's trainer, Eddie Futch, who instructed his fighter to aim for Ali's body. Instead Norton ended up breaking Ali's jaw in the second round. Ali did not want the fight stopped. He fought for the full 12 rounds and lost by a split decision—a 2 to 1 vote of the judges.

Hecklers called out: "That loudmouth is finished!" Ali received a note that read: "The butterfly has lost its wings, the bee has lost its sting." It took six months for his jaw to heal, and then he faced Norton again.

This time Ali trained harder and took Norton more seriously. The effort paid off. He won the fight with his jab, victorious by a unanimous decision. He fought once more that year, winning a decision over Rudi Lubbers in Jakarta, Indonesia, in October.

More than anything, Ali wanted a rematch with Joe Frazier. Frazier had fought only twice that year and had lost the title to 25-year-old George Foreman in Kingston, Jamaica, in January 1973. Foreman had knocked Frazier down six times in two rounds before the referee stopped the fight.

In January 1974, Ali and Frazier finally met again. Although it was not a world title fight, it was a fight that would redeem Ali and one that the fans wanted to see. The two fighters faced each other in Madison Square Garden with each man guaranteed $850,000 by the promoter. The Garden was sold out. Ali was a slight favorite.

This fight was very different from the first one. Ali, in much better condition than before, moved quickly around

Ali shares a joke with Johnny Carson on The Tonight Show.

the ring and defused most of Frazier's power and punches by holding him. Both fighters threw far fewer punches than they had before. At the end of the 12th round, Ali was the winner by unanimous decision.

Now, it was Frazier's turn to ask for a rematch. But Ali wanted the heavyweight title back first. He needed to fight George Foreman to get it.

"The Rumble in the Jungle" would take place in Africa—in Kinshasa, Zaire—that October. The bout, organized by the government of Zaire and boxing promoter Don King, was originally scheduled for September 25. But Foreman cut his eye while sparring, postponing the bout until October 30. Each fighter would receive $5 million. Foreman was the favorite to win and, like his hero, Sonny Liston, was considered unbeatable.

He was 26 years old, from Marshall, Texas, with a record of 40 wins, 37 knockouts, and no losses. A neighborhood troublemaker, he had joined the Youth Corps as a teenager and then had turned to boxing. He won the Olympic heavyweight gold medal in 1968 in Mexico City. He was a tremendous puncher with both hands.

In Zaire, Foreman remained in seclusion. He traveled with police dogs and had food and water flown in from the United States. He couldn't wait to get home—away from all the publicity. "I am the most boring man in the world," he said at a press conference.

Ali, on the other hand, promoted himself and the fight, granting interviews, attending press conferences, and signing autographs. "It's a great feeling being in a country operated by black people." Ali told reporters.

The crowds were overwhelmingly in favor of Ali. People lined the streets, eager to see him and to run with him in the mornings. "Ali—Kill him!" was written on posters and pasted on fences.

The fight started at 3:00 A.M., so it could be broadcast live back in the United States. "Ali! Kill him!" shouted the crowd as Ali entered the ring. In the early rounds, the powerful Foreman pursued Ali around the ring and pinned him against the ropes. Ali used his "rope-a-dope" technique: he covered his head and let Foreman hit him in the body and wear himself out. Ali taunted Foreman: "Is that all you've got, Big George? Don't you know who I am?"

The crowd was surprised that Ali could hold up to so much power. But Foreman became tired in the seventh round. In the eighth, Ali threw a hard left and then a right and Foreman went down. Foreman had run out of gas. Ali knocked him out with a barrage of punches.

"The first round, his punches hurt. It was boom! boom! boom!" Ali said. "Second round, they hurt less. And after a while, they were coming in real slow and not too hard." Ali raised his hands in his famous pose of victory. Angelo Dundee and Bundini Brown jumped for joy and hugged Ali. Spectators climbed into the ring. Ali had finally regained his title.

He was named Fighter of the Year by *Ring* magazine and Sportsman of the Year by *Sports Illustrated*. Once considered a traitor to his country, Ali even received an

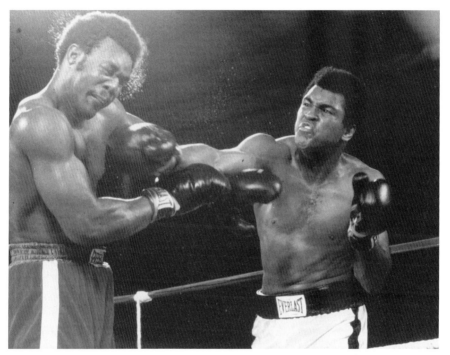

"The Rumble in the Jungle"—Ali rocks Foreman.

invitation to the White House to visit with President Gerald Ford.

Moving toward a rematch with Frazier in 1975, Ali defended his title successfully three more times. He stopped Chuck Wepner in the 15th round and Ron Lyle in the 11th, and he won a unanimous decision over Joe Bugner.

Next, the rematch with Joe Frazier, "the Thrilla in Manila." Ali recited:

It will be a killer
And a chiller
And a thriller
When I get the gorilla
In Manila.

Ali punched and punched a large stuffed gorilla in the ring at his Deer Lake training camp. "Joe Frazier, Joe Frazier," he repeated in front of a large crowd and television cameras.

At a press conference before the fight, Ali leaned across the table at his opponent. "I'm gonna do something to you," he warned, pretending to hit Frazier, who looked back in amusement. "I promise I'll hit you on the head the most."

He playfully hit a black plastic gorilla and shouted to the crowd: "Gotta capture the gorilla! Joe Frazier's face is so ugly that it should be donated to the Bureau of Wildlife!"

Frazier, meanwhile, was out for revenge. "I'm going to make him quit. No matter what name he goes by, he's gonna quit," he insisted. Frazier's eldest son, Marvis, who was 14 at the time, accompanied his father to Manila, in the Philippines, for the much-anticipated bout.

"I was upset and confused," Marvis Frazier recalls. "This guy [Ali] was supposed to be a black leader, he was supposed to be for brotherhood and for God. But God didn't go out and call people names. Pop was the everyday, working man, always humble. The other guy had the lip.

Ali, being a black man, maybe he had an identity crisis. My father didn't have to prove that he was black."

In the Philippines, billboards advertised "The Fight of a Lifetime." Ali was the center of attention—not because of his stand on the Vietnam War or his religion, but because of his personal life. Muhammad and Belinda Ali had been married for eight years. But Ali brought another woman, Veronica Porche, to the fight. Ferdinand Marcos, president of the Philippines, assumed that Porche was Ali's wife, and Ali didn't correct the president's mistake.

Reporters pounced on the story, which became a major topic of discussion. Ali shrugged off the criticism. "I know celebrities don't have privacy," Ali said, addressing the issue at a press conference, "but at least they should be able to sleep with who they want. They shouldn't be able to get on me for having a girlfriend."

Muhammad had met Veronica while preparing for the Foreman fight. She had won a beauty contest to become one of four "poster girls" hired to promote the event. Muhammad had fallen in love with her. No longer shy around women, he also had two young daughters, Miya and Khaliah, born to women other than his wife.

When the news about Veronica Porche became public, Belinda Ali, wearing a flowing white dress and white turban, flew from Chicago to Manila. With the press tagging behind her, she proceeded to her husband's hotel room. A noisy argument followed. Then Belinda turned right around and flew back home to Chicago. She and Muhammad were close to divorce.

Despite the turmoil in his personal life, Ali focused on the Thrilla in Manila. About 770 million viewers would watch the fight on television. Ali would earn $6 million and Frazier $3 million, regardless of who won or lost. Ali was favored to win.

President Marcos and his wife, Imelda, were seated ringside. "Smokin' Joe" was inscribed on the back of Frazier's robe. When Ali was introduced, he raised his hands and walked around the ring as the crowd shouted his name. The fighters talked to each other from the opening bell, with both men punching from the start.

Frazier had Ali on the ropes in the third round. Ali's hands went up to protect his face and head. Then, he suddenly whipped his hands out and started punching Frazier's head. The fight went back and forth: Frazier assaulting and then retreating, Ali assaulting and then retreating. Ali dominated in the beginning, Frazier in the middle, and Ali at the end. They both looked exhausted.

Ali could barely come out for the 13th round. He tried to knock Frazier out, throwing nonstop punches to Frazier's face and body. Frazier, wobbly, refused to go down. They both walked slowly to their corners. Frazier was bleeding badly from inside his mouth, and his left eye was completely closed. He had difficulty seeing out of his right eye, and he was spitting blood.

Before the bell rang for the 15th round, Frazier's trainer, Eddie Futch, asked his fighter how he felt. "I can see his left but not his right," Frazier responded.

"Sit down, son. It's all over," Futch said compassionately.

"But no one will ever forget what you did here today."
Not wanting to see his fighter permanently injured, Futch
threw in the towel. For Ali, who had to be helped out of
the ring to his dressing room, the end of the fight "was
like death. Closest thing to dyin' that I know of."

Although badly battered, he was still the victor. "Kids
would draw little stick figures," Marvis Frazier remembers. "The stick figure with his hands up was Ali and the
figure on the ground was my father."

Frazier begins to crumble.

Relaxing with daughters Laila and Hana, 1978

CALLING IT QUITS

ALI WAS 34 YEARS OLD IN 1976—NOT OLD IN THE general sense, but old in the boxing world, where the reflexes of a 20-year-old are greatly valued. As a fighter gets older, his legs move more slowly, his reflexes are not as fast. He can see a punch coming but he can't react as quickly as he used to. He knows all the techniques, but his legs and his punches no longer have as much snap to them. He can't move out of the way of oncoming punches.

It happens to all fighters and it happened to Ali. Some retire, unable to keep up with the younger crowd and fearful of being injured. Others, like Ali, continue to fight.

Ali defended his title four times that year, knocking out Jean Pierre Coopman, beating Jimmy Young by decision, stopping Richard Dunn, and meeting Ken Norton for a third time—this time winning a 15-round decision. In this fight, he was not the Ali of old—he was slower, more tentative, and he did not punch as hard. He spent more time moving around than throwing punches. When the decision was announced, Norton held his head in his hands. "I thought it was a terrible decision," he said.

Muhammad and Belinda Ali divorced in September 1976. His four children remained with their mother in Chicago. Muhammad moved in with Veronica Porche and they had a daughter, Hana. When the baby was 10 months old, Muhammad and Veronica got married in Los Angeles. They honeymooned in Hawaii.

Ali defended his title twice in 1977, winning 15-round decisions over both Alfredo Evangelista and Earnie Shavers, one of the hardest hitting punchers in the heavyweight division. Ali absorbed more punches than he had in the past. But he was still good enough to beat these opponents.

His next opponent would be 24-year-old Leon Spinks. The fight was scheduled for February 1978. Spinks was not expected to give Ali any trouble, mostly because of his undisciplined and inconsistent training habits. Spinks and his older brother, Michael, had both won medals at the 1976 Olympics in Montreal. The idea of beating another Olympic medalist intrigued Ali. He had beaten gold medalists Patterson, Frazier, and Foreman.

Spinks, born in East St. Louis, Illinois, and raised by his mother, was a former Marine and a respected amateur fighter. After the Olympics, in 1977, Spinks turned pro.

Before he fought Ali, his record was 6-0, with one draw against Scott LeDoux. This would be his eighth fight. If he won, his victory would be one of the biggest upsets in boxing history.

Ali called Spinks "Dracula" because his front teeth were missing. Even though Ali hadn't fought in five months, he didn't take his young challenger seriously. At age 36, not watching his weight as he normally did, he weighed 242 pounds. He had worked out less and had sparred (held practice fights) for just 20 rounds. Spinks was in shape, well conditioned, and ready.

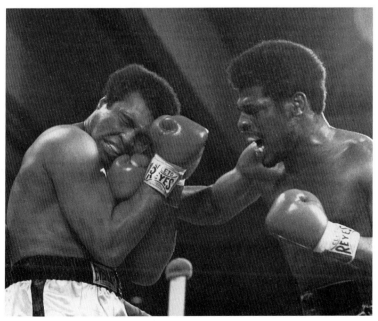

Ali versus Spinks: now the tables are turned.

Ali took Spinks lightly for the first six rounds, expecting his young opponent to tire. But it never happened. Although Spinks was a wild puncher, Ali was not in good enough shape to move out of the way. His own punches had very little power. Spinks remained fresh throughout the fight and stunned the boxing world by winning a 15-round split decision. It was Spinks' night of triumph.

"I just couldn't leave boxing that way, losing an embarrassing fight like that," Ali said afterward. "Leon Spinks borrowed my title, that's all." He demanded a rematch.

In June 1978, Ali traveled throughout the Soviet Union, where he made headlines, signed autographs, and greeted the Soviet people. He met with Soviet leader Leonid Brezhnev and discussed U.S.-Soviet relations. He was as popular there as he was in the United States. Everyone wanted to meet him.

Back home, Ali trained hard for his rematch with Spinks, to be held in September in New Orleans, Louisiana. He pushed himself in training, running three to five miles before breakfast every day and sparring for more than 200 rounds.

In front of more than 60,000 people in the New Orleans Superdome, Ali was in command from the opening round. He jabbed Spinks all night long, never letting him become aggressive. Spinks lacked the fire that he had had in the first fight. Ali backpedaled and even did his rope-a-dope in the final round. Spinks' punches kept missing. At age 36, Ali recaptured his title by a unanimous decision.

"He was always my idol," Spinks said afterward. "He

still is. I beat the man and then the man beat me. That's all there is to say." Ali became the first man in boxing history to win the world heavyweight championship three times.

Finally, in 1979, Muhammad Ali announced his retirement. After 19 years and 59 professional bouts, it was time to call it quits. By that time, Muhammad and Veronica had a second daughter, Laila. The family lived in Los Angeles. Their home was a museumlike mansion that included seven bedrooms, a library, and a billiard parlor.

The three-time champion, 1979

Ali went on a lecture tour. He endorsed Idaho potatoes and other products and appeared in a four-hour television miniseries called *Freedom Road*. Ali played an ex-slave and Civil War veteran who eventually becomes a United States senator. Singer and actor Kris Kristofferson costarred in the series. He played a southern sharecropper.

Ali plays the part of Gideon Jackson in Freedom Road.

Next, Ali traveled to Bangladesh and rode in a motorcade through crowded streets. "These are my people," he said, as fans trotted after him. Songs were sung in tribute. He rode elephants and playfully sparred with children.

"Mr. Ambassador," as Ali was sometimes called, then went to Africa at the request of President Jimmy Carter to drum up support for the U.S. boycott of the 1980 Olympics. The Games were scheduled for Moscow, in the Soviet Union, and the boycott stemmed from opposition to the Soviet invasion of Afghanistan. Ali visited with leaders in Tanzania, Kenya, Nairobi, Nigeria, Liberia, and Senegal and explained the U.S. position on the boycott. The trip was not very successful—many African nations supported the Soviet Union. But as usual, Ali was a hit. He playfully fought with the smiling crowd.

Retirement didn't last very long. After Ali stepped down, Larry Holmes became the heavyweight champion by beating Ken Norton in a 15-round decision. Ali thought he could beat the 28-year-old Holmes easily. He knew Holmes and his style of boxing because the two fighters had sparred with each other at Deer Lake. Holmes felt that he had to beat Ali in order to gain the respect of the boxing community.

So, two years after his last fight and for his 60th bout, the 38-year-old champion came out of retirement. "He's only Larry Holmes and he's nothin'," said Ali. "Holmes must go. I'll eat him up. Holmes can't beat me."

"If Ali stays in front of me, he's going to get knocked out early," returned Holmes. "Now he's going to find out

*Ali with his third
wife, Veronica*

how it feels to be an old man fighting a good fast young
man. Ali will fall," he predicted. "The old man is in big
trouble. Ali had his day—this is my day."

Most people on Ali's staff thought that he shouldn't
fight Holmes. Ali was beginning to have health problems.
He sometimes slurred his speech and didn't always seem
alert. He occasionally fell asleep during interviews. People wondered if Ali had "punch-drunkenness," a deterio-
ration of the brain caused by blows to the head and
common to boxers.

A medical evalution by the Mayo Clinic in Rochester, Minnesota, revealed that Ali was in poor health. But the Nevada State Athletic Commission approved the fight—to be held in Las Vegas in October 1980.

Ali weighed in at 217, Holmes at 211. For the first few rounds, Ali looked fantastic. He had lost 43 pounds—coming down from 260—and he moved quickly. But his punches weren't strong ones.

Holmes was respectful of Ali for the first five rounds, not attacking as hard as he could have. And then the fight became painful to watch. This was not the same fighter who had fought Liston, Patterson, Foreman, and Frazier. Ali's punches were tentative ones, while Holmes performed at his best.

At home in Hancock Park, Los Angeles

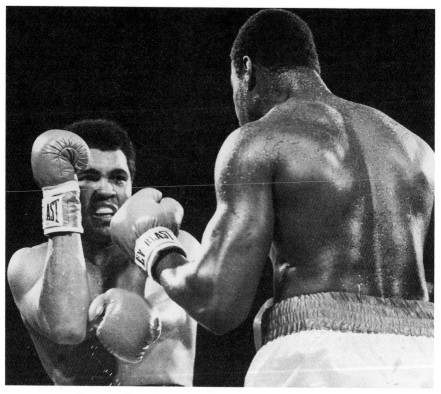

Larry Holmes erased any hopes of another comeback.

The judges awarded every round to Holmes. He had tears in his eyes. He had beaten the Greatest, who didn't look that great anymore. "We gotta be honest," said Ali to Holmes at the press conference after the fight, "You won clean and fair. Give him support until I return," he advised the crowd.

A little more than a year later, Ali fought again to see what skills he had left. "I would like Muhammad to stop because he's got nothing to prove," said trainer Angelo Dundee. But Ali disagreed: "You know it's time to leave but something tells you you've got to take one more gamble."

Trevor Berbick was considered an easy opponent, a 29-year-old contender from Jamaica who had lost a 15-round decision to Larry Holmes eight months earlier. "I'm gonna mess 'em all up by whupping Berbick and then becoming the first forty-year-old man to ever win the heavyweight title. Get ready for the shocker," Ali warned. "I'm gonna mess up the world."

The matchup with Berbick, held in Nassau, in the Bahamas, on December 11, 1981, was not highly publicized. The fight started several hours late because the promoters had not brought boxing gloves with them. The gloves had to be flown in from Miami.

Ali, at age 39, weighed 236—19 pounds more than when he had fought Holmes. Berbick, an awkward fighter who was difficult to hit, was not much of a puncher. But he was the aggressor throughout the 10 rounds. Berbick won by decision. This fight would be Ali's last. It was a sad finale to a brilliant career.

"Father Time caught up with me," Ali announced. "I'm finished."

"I Ain't Dead Yet!"

AFTER HE QUIT BOXING FOR GOOD, ALI TRAVELED around the world, making personal appearances and spreading the word of the Nation of Islam. He endorsed products and promoted boxing matches for a year or two.

But his health continued to decline. Doctors diagnosed his condition as Parkinson's syndrome, a degenerative brain disorder. He began to move and speak very slowly. His hands trembled and his face often looked blank. Many doctors believe that Ali's condition was caused by repeated blows to the head.

Ali's fortune had also declined. He had earned tens of millions of dollars in the ring. He donated hundreds of thousands to charities, people in need, and the Nation of Islam. Millions more had been lost on bad investments.

Numerous business ventures, including a line of clothing called Muhammad Ali Sportswear, had failed.

His marriage to Veronica Porche also failed. In 1986, the couple divorced. Ali quickly remarried, this time to Lonnie Williams, a Muslim woman who had grown up on his street in Louisville. She was just a little girl when Olympic champion Cassius Clay visited and played with the kids in the neighborhood.

Ali continued to visit Williams and her family every time he went to Louisville. Even as she grew up and went off to college, she and Muhammad stayed in touch. After graduating from college, Lonnie moved to Los Angeles and converted to Islam, which brought her even closer to Muhammad.

"What happened was, our friendship had become very strong," she said, "which is the way I think all marriages should start." On November 19, 1986, the couple was married. The ceremony was small—just 20 people attended the wedding. Muhammad and Lonnie adopted a son, Asaad, a few years later.

Altogether, Ali has nine children. He didn't spend as much time with his children as other fathers did; he was usually training, fighting, or traveling. For the children, life with a famous father wasn't always easy. Ali's divorces and extramarital affairs were well publicized. When he divorced Belinda and later Veronica, he was also separated from his children by those marriages. Miya and Khaliah, his daughters outside of marriage, spent even less time with their father.

Most of Ali's children are now grown and live in different cities around the United States. "I didn't have as much time as I wanted to teach them. . . . I wasn't really around to raise them," Ali says.

Ali gets a hug from his daughter Maryum in 1988. The robe was a gift from Elvis Presley.

Laila Ali stares down her opponent before knocking her out in the first round of her pro boxing debut fight.

But Ali's second-youngest daughter, Laila, has followed in his footsteps and started her own career in boxing.

"Right now, people don't know me," she told *People* in 1999. "They say, 'we'll see what she can do.' Well, I can't wait to get in the ring and show them."

Laila seems to have her father's talent as well as his confidence. At the age of 21, she won her professional boxing debut with a knockout 31 seconds into the first round. She went on to win three more fights by knockout, an impressive beginning that made her father proud.

"You're good," her father told her as she sparred with him during a 1999 interview with *People.* "I don't have to give you any pointers."

Ali's finances are reported to be sound once again, and his health is fair. "People say I talk so slow today. That's no surprise," he says. "I calculate I've taken 29,000 punches, but I earned [millions of dollars] and I saved half of it. I may talk slow, but my mind is okay."

"Muhammad is very healthy," says Lonnie Ali. "He's still as quick witted as he always was. He's more introspective now. He's very much a Muslim."

Muhammad, Lonnie, and Asaad live a comfortable life, with a home in Los Angeles and a small farm in Berrien Springs, Michigan, northeast of Chicago. The Deer Lake training camp, its boulders still painted with the names of great fighters, is leased to a home for single mothers for only a dollar a year.

Ali wakes up at five o'clock each morning to recite the morning Muslim prayer. He signs religious pamphlets that read "Introducing Islam" and "God Is One" and distributes them to the crowds that gather around him.

"Allah said to me, 'I made you the most famous man in the world, gave you fame and riches and friends from all walks of life,'" he said. "So now I do this for him."

More than 20 years after he left the boxing ring, Ali continues to make appearances, and crowds still gather for autographs and a look at the Greatest. He personally answers every fan letter that he receives—hundreds each month. As he did at Deer Lake, he welcomes fans, neighbors, and friends to his home. He never turns down a request for an autograph.

Ali makes a limited number of public appearances, occasionally showing up ringside at major title fights. He makes news whenever he travels and still serves as an unofficial ambassador for the United States. In November 1990, he traveled to Iraq to meet with Iraqi leader Saddam Hussein, a fellow Muslim, who was holding 300 Americans captive in the months leading up to the Persian Gulf War. Ali hoped to negotiate for their release. He was partially successful, returning to the United States ten days later with 15 Americans.

He then traveled to the Sudan in Africa as part of an Islamic relief mission. He gently held starving children as doctors examined them. He flew to India, met with Mother Teresa, and visited hospitals and orphanages. In May 1994, he accompanied the families of American servicemen, missing since the Vietnam War, to meet families of missing Vietnamese servicemen. "People who were bitter enemies toward each other sat down and came to terms and made peace," he said. "It's a great thing to be here to witness this."

At his televised 50th birthday party in 1992, Ali received standing ovations from the star-studded crowd. "When I was born, Muhammad Ali was the heavyweight champion," said singer Whitney Houston. "I've never had a world without Muhammad Ali."

In Saudi Arabia, early 1990s. Ali, wife Lonnie (behind him), and manager Herbert Muhammad (right), visit the Muslim holy land.

"Muhammad Ali is a man whose life is devoted to shattering stereotypes," said singer MC Hammer, who called Ali's poetry the root of rap.

An emotional Howard Cosell said, "You never wavered. You're free to be who you want to be. I love you."

When Joe Frazier walked to the podium to pay his tribute, Ali jumped from his seat and raised his fists—pretending to threaten his former rival. The crowd roared with laughter. Although he moved slowly, the champion was still every bit the showman.

Muhammad Ali has been called the most beloved and socially significant athlete in history. He is one of the most photographed and interviewed personalities in the world of sports. He has been the subject of more books and articles than nearly any other athlete. His opponents took the spotlight, too, receiving more attention and more money than they did when they fought someone else.

A museum honoring Ali opened in May 1995 in a large room in a shopping mall in downtown Louisville. Trophies, robes, documents—including Ali's original six-

Ali lights the Olympic flame for the 1996 Summer Olympic Games in Atlanta while U.S. swimmer Janet Evans looks on.

page, typewritten letter requesting exemption from military service—fill the room.

In 1996, Ali was chosen to light the Olympic flame at the Summer Games in Atlanta. It was an honor for Ali to be able to light the torch in Martin Luther King's hometown. Before Ali left the stadium, President Clinton told him, "They didn't tell me who would light the flame, but when I saw it was you, I cried."

In his professional career, Ali was never knocked out, retiring after 61 bouts with a record of 56 wins, 37 knockouts, and just five losses. He was the first and only man to win the heavyweight title three times.

Many younger fighters have modeled themselves after Muhammad Ali. Some show off poor imitations of the Ali shuffle and the rope-a-dope. But there has never been one who could match up. Ali set the standard by which all boxers are judged.

Trainer George Benton, who worked with Leon Spinks during the first Ali-Spinks fight, summed up Ali's spirit this way: "Liston, Foreman, Frazier. The draft thing. Ali always comes up on his feet. It's like there's some mystical force guiding his life, making him not like other men."

USA Today named Muhammad Ali "Athlete of the Century" in 1999, and *Sports Illustrated* awarded him a similar honor. Yet Ali's work is still not done.

The Greatest himself concludes: "People said that I had a full life, but I ain't dead yet. There's bigger work I got to do. The whole world is in trouble. My main goal now is helping people and preparing for the hereafter."

B I B L I O G R A P H Y

Ali, Muhammad, and Richard Durham. *The Greatest: My Own Story.* London: Hart-Davis, MacGibbon, 1976.

———. *Muhammad Ali in His Own Words.* New York: Pinnacle Books, 1975.

Bingham, Howard L. *Muhammad Ali: A Thirty-Year Journey.* New York: Simon & Schuster, 1993.

Cope, Myron. *Broken Cigars.* Englewood Cliffs, N.J.: Prentice-Hall, 1968.

Cottrell, John. *Muhammad Ali, Who Once Was Cassius Clay.* New York: Funk & Wagnalls, 1968.

Eyes on the Prize II: America at the Racial Crossroads, 1965 to 1985, "Ain't Gonna Shuffle No More (1964-1972)." Boston: Blackside, Inc., 1989. Videorecording.

Gelman, Steve. *Young Olympic Champions.* New York: Norton, 1964.

Hauser, Thomas. *Muhammad Ali: His Life and Times.* New York: Simon & Schuster, 1991.

Kindred, Dave. "He'll Always Be The Greatest." *The Sporting News,* July 29, 1996, 6.

Leifer, Neil. *Muhammad Ali Memories.* New York: Rizzoli, 1992.

Lewis, Claude. *Cassius Clay: A No-Holds-Barred Biography of Boxing's Most Controversial Champion.* New York: Macfadden-Bartell Corp., 1965.

Lipsyte, Robert. *Free To Be Muhammad Ali.* New York: Bantam Books, 1978.

Mailer, Norman. *The Fight.* Boston: Little Brown, 1975.

——. *Norman Mailer on the Fight of the Century.* New York: New American Library, 1971.

Muhammad Ali: Fiftieth Birthday Celebration. ABC-TV, March 1, 1992.

Mullan, Harry, ed. *The Book of Boxing Quotations.* London: Stanley Paul, 1991.

Nack, William. "Young Cassius Clay." *Sports Illustrated,* January 13, 1992, 70-81.

Olsen, Jack. *Black Is Best: The Riddle of Cassius Clay.* New York: Putnam, 1967.

Pacheco, Ferdie. *Muhammad Ali: A View From the Corner.* New York: Carol Publishing Group, 1992.

Sheed, Wilfrid. *Muhammad Ali: A Portrait in Words and Photographs.* New York: Crowell, 1975.

Sugar, Bert Randolph. *The Great Fights: A Pictorial History of Boxing's Greatest Bouts.* New York: Rutledge Press, 1981.

——, ed. *The Ring Record Book and Boxing Encyclopedia.* New York: Atheneum, 1981.

Sullivan, George. *The Cassius Clay Story.* New York: Fleet Publishing Corp., 1964.

Torres, Jose. *Sting Like a Bee: The Muhammad Ali Story.* New York: Abelard-Schuman, n.d.

Tresniowski, Alex and Kelly Carter. "In His Image." *People Weekly,* April 26, 1999, 103–105.

I N D E X

Other paperback editions in the BIOGRAPHY® series:

A B O U T   T H E   A U T H O R

Arlene Schulman is a journalist and photojournalist living in New York City. Her articles and photographs have appeared in the *New York Times, Inside Sports, Sport,* and other publications. *The Prizefighters,* a book featuring her award-winning photographs, was published in 1994. *Muhammad Ali* is her first book for young readers.

PHOTO ACKNOWLEDGMENTS

Photographs are used with permission of: Archive Photos, pp. 2, 10, 38-39, 40, 58, 75, 102, 105; © Bettmann/Corbis, pp. 6, 9, 12, 14, 17, 22, 24, 26, 31, 37, 42, 47, 49, 53, 54, 56, 57, 60, 64, 66, 70, 78, 80, 82, 85, 86, 88, 91, 95, 99, 106, 108, 111, 118-119; Archive Photos/ Popperfoto, pp. 19, 44, 45; THE RING magazine, p. 34; Archive Photos/Express Newspapers, pp. 51, 73, 96, 104, 115; Archive Photos/American Stock, p. 77; Archive Photos/Fotos International, p. 101; AP/Wide World Photos, pp. 112, 116; © Allsport/MSI, p. 120; © Allsport, p 128.

Cover photos: © Allsport/MSI, front and back cover.
Author photo: Marc Bryan-Brown